Basic Instructions for Cutting, Sewing,
Layering, Quilting and Binding are
on pages 24 - 27

TIPS: As a Guide for Yardage:
Each ¼ yard or a 'Fat Quarter' equals 3 strips.
A pre-cut 'Jelly Roll' strip is 2½" x 44".
Cut 'Fat Quarter' and yardage strips to 2½" x 22".

Yardage is given for using either
fabric yardage or 'Jelly Roll' strips.

Th

Jelly Rolls
Non-Fattening
Sugar Free
No Cholesterol

Index

Flowers in the Garden

pieced by Donna Perrotta
quilted by Julie Lawson

It's a beautiful day in this neighborhood of stately homes with lovingly planted flower gardens and it will be a beautiful day in your sewing room as these simple blocks grow into a fabulous family favorite.

instructions on pages 13 - 15

Butterflies & Dragonflies
Dandelion Girl

pieced by Kayleen Allen
quilted by Sue Needle

Enliven your decor with gentle flutterings on soft pastels. This flock of butterflies is migrating to your sewing room right now. You won't need a net to catch the fun of creating this gorgeous quilt.

instructions on pages 16 - 18

Garden Inspirations

pieced by Kayleen Allen
quilted by Julie Lawson

Rich, sumptuous colors make this a perfect gift for the men in your family. While luxurious earth-tones complement the decor in modern homes, the traditional blocks and clean lines will please those leaning toward both Victorian and country decor.
instructions on pages 19 - 23

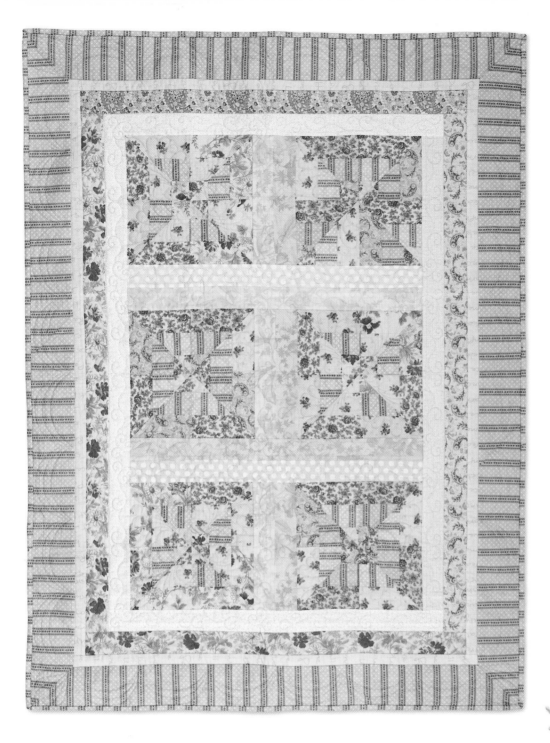

Simplicity

pieced by Kayleen Allen
quilted by Julie Lawson

Soften any space in your home with pretty pastels in gentle colors. This is the quilt you want to come home to after a hard day. Curl up in your favorite chair with these soothing textures.
instructions on pages 11 - 12

Simplicity

photo on page 10

SIZE: 44" x 59"

YARDAGE:

We used a *Moda* "Simplicity" by 3 Sisters
  'Jelly Roll' collection of 2½" fabric strips
  - we purchased 1 'Jelly Roll'

⅓ yard White	OR	4 strips
½ yard Green	OR	6 strips
½ yard Aqua	OR	6 strips
½ yard Pink	OR	7 strips
½ yard Yellow	OR	7 strips

Border #1	Purchase ⅙ yard Light Pink
Border #2 & Binding	Purchase 1 yard Green
Backing	Purchase 2½ yards
Batting	Purchase 52" x 67"

Sewing machine, needle, thread

PREPARATION FOR BLOCKS

Sew 3 strips of Green together side by side to make a piece 6½" wide. Press.
Sew 3 strips of Pink together side by side to make a piece 6½" wide. Press.
Sew 3 strips of Aqua together side by side to make a piece 6½" wide. Press.
Sew 3 strips of Yellow together side by side to make a piece 6½" wide. Press.
Cut each strip into 6 blocks 6½" x 6½".

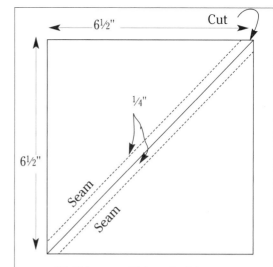

Half-Square Triangle Diagram
1. Place 2 squares right sides together.
2. Draw a diagonal line from corner to corner.
3. Stitch ¼" on each side of the line.
4. Cut squares apart on the diagonal line.
5. Open the 2 new squares with 2 colors.
6. Press. Trim off dog-ears.
7. Trim to 6" x 6".

SEW HALF-SQUARE TRIANGLES:

Pair each Green block with a Pink block, right sides together.
Pair each Aqua block with a Yellow block, right sides together.

Follow the instructions in the Half-Square Triangle Diagram.

Each block will measure 6" x 6" at this point.

Green - Pink
Half-square
Triangle Blocks
Make 12 each

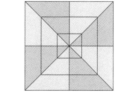

Green - Pink
Pinwheel Block
Make 3

SEW BLOCKS:

Arrange pieces to form each Pinwheel block.
Sew 2 half-square triangles together to make each row.
Sew 2 rows together to finish each block.
Make 6 blocks.
Each block will measure 11½" x 11½" at this point.

Aqua - Yellow
Half-square Triangle Blocks
Make 12 each

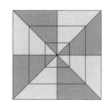

Aqua - Yellow
Pinwheel Block
Make 3

SASHING STRIPS:

Vertical Rows: Cut 3 Pink and 3 Green 2½" x 11½"
  Sew together side by side in pairs -
  Pink to Green. Press.

Horizontal Rows: Cut 2 Aqua, 1 Yellow, and
  1 Pink strip 2½" x 26½".
For row 2, sew an Aqua to a Yellow strip. Press.
For row 4, sew an Aqua to a Pink strip. Press.

ASSEMBLE THE CENTER SECTION:

Arrange all Blocks and Sashing strips on a work surface or table.
Refer to diagram for placement and direction.

Rows:
Sew blocks together in 3 rows, 2 blocks and 1 pair of Vertical sashing strips per row. Press.
Sew all 5 rows together. Press.

Row 1
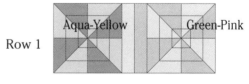

Row 2

Row 3

Row 4

Row 5
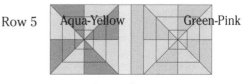

Center Section

ADD THE BORDERS:
White Pieced Border #1:
> Cut 2 strips 2½" x 41½" for sides.
> Cut 2 strips 2½" x 30½" for top and bottom.
> Sew side borders to the quilt. Press.
> Sew top and bottom borders to the quilt. Press.

Pieced Border #2:
> Cut 1 Yellow and 1 Pink strip 2½" x 45½" for
> > sides.
> Cut 1 Yellow and 1 Pink strip 2½" x 34½" for top
> > and bottom.
> Sew side borders to the quilt. Press.
> Sew top and bottom borders to the quilt. Press.

Border #3:
Cut 1½" strips.
Sew strips together end to end.
> Cut 2 strips 1½" x 49½" for sides.
> Cut 2 strips 1½" x 36½" for top and bottom.
> Sew side borders to the quilt. Press.
> Sew top and bottom borders to the quilt. Press.

Mitered Border #4:
Cut 4½" strips.
Sew strips together end to end.
> Cut 2 strips 4½" x 61½" for sides.
> Cut 2 strips 4½" x 46½" for top and bottom.
> Follow the instructions for mitered borders.

FINISHING:
Quilting:
> See Basic Instructions on pages 26 - 28.
Binding:
> Cut five 2½" strips.
> > Sew together end to end to equal 214".
> > See Binding Instructions on page 27.

Simplicity
Quilt Assembly Diagram

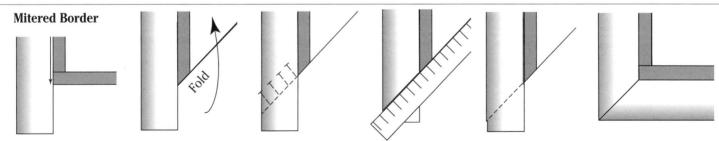

Mitered Border

Center, pin and sew borders to the sides of the quilt. Stop the seam at the corner.

Fold the quilt at a diagonal so the miter will extend from the corner outward.

Pin or baste miter seam, carefully, lining up the pattern.

Use a ruler to draw a line from the corner out to the edge of the border. Sew a seam.
TIP: I use a long stitch in case I need to rip it out and redo it.

Check the miter seam to be sure it lines up correctly and lays down flat, resew it with a normal stitch.

Trim off excess fabric underneath the corners. Repeat on all 4 corners.

Flowers in the Garden

photos on pages 4 - 5

SIZE: 52" x 60"

YARDAGE:

We used a *Moda* "Summer's Basket of Flowers"
by Terry Thompson
'Jelly Roll' collection of 2½" fabric strips
- we purchased 1 'Jelly Roll'

⅓ yard Red	OR	4 strips
⅔ yard Ivory	OR	9 strips
½ yard Gold	OR	7 strips
⅓ yard Brown	OR	5 strips
½ yard Blue	OR	7 strips
⅝ yard Green	OR	8 strips

Border #2	Purchase ¼ yard Red
Border #3 & Binding	Purchase 1⅛ yards Gold
Backing	Purchase 3 yards
Batting	Purchase 60" x 68"

Sewing machine, needle, thread

PREPARATION FOR BLOCKS:

House 1:

Cut 3 Blue and 2 Brown squares 2½" x 2½" for chimneys.
Cut 1 Gold and 3 Brown strips 2½" x 10½" for roof and wall.
Cut 2 Brown 2½" x 2½" squares, 2 Gold strips 1½" x 2½" and 1 Gold strip 2½" x 4½" for window sections.
Cut 1 Brown strip 2½" x 6½" for the door.
Cut 4 Gold strips 2½" x 6½" for walls.
Cut 2 Blue strips 2½" x 18½" for sides (#22 & #23).
Arrange the pieces following the House 1 Diagram.
    Sew the pieces for each row together side by side. Press.
Sew strips #1-2-3-4-5 together for windows section.
Sew strips #6-7-8-9-10 together for door section.
Sew strips #11-12-13-14-15 together for chimneys section.

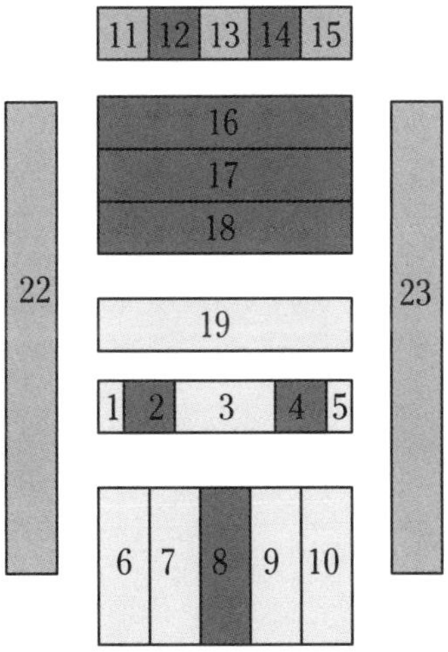

Sew the rows together in numerical sequence. Press.
Sew strips #22 and 23 to each side of the block. Press.

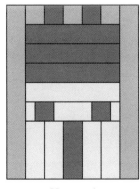

House 1

House 2:

Cut 2 Blue squares 2½" x 2½" for chimney.
Cut 1 Brown strip 2½" x 6½" for chimney.
Cut 2 Gold and 2 Brown strips 2½" x 10½" for roof and upper floor.
Cut 3 Brown and 3 Gold squares 2½" x 2½" for windows.
Cut 1 Brown strip 2½" x 6½" for the door.
Cut 3 Gold strips 2½" x 6½" and 1 Gold 2½" x 4½" for walls.
Cut 2 Blue strips 2½" x 18½" for sides (#19 & #20).
Arrange the pieces following the House 2 Diagram.
    Sew the pieces for each row together. Press.
Sew the rows together in numerical order. Press.
Sew a Blue 18½" strip to each side of the block. Press.

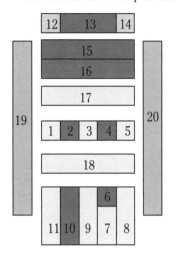

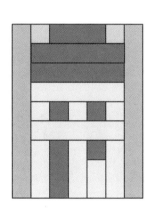

House 2

House 3:

Cut the following 2½" wide Blue strips for the sky:
    two 4½", two 2½".
Cut 1 Brown strip 2½" x 2½" for chimney.
Cut 2 Brown strips 2½" x 10½" and 1 strip 2½" x 6½" for roof.
Cut 3 Brown and 4 Gold squares 2½" x 2½" for windows.
Cut 1 Brown strip 2½" x 6½" for the door.
Cut 3 Gold strips 2½" x 12½" and 1 Gold 2½" x 4½" for walls.
Arrange the pieces following the House 3 Diagram.
    Sew the pieces for each row together. Press.
Sew the rows together in numerical order. Press.

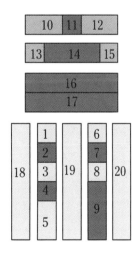

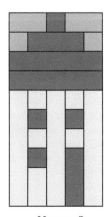

House 3

Flowers in the Garden - continued from page 13

Half-Square
Triangle
Make 12

PINWHEEL FLOWER BLOCKS:

Pinwheel Flowers:

Cut 3 Red and 3 Ivory strips 2½" x 39½".

For each color, sew 3 strips together side by side to make a piece 6½" x 39½".

Cut each piece into 6 squares 6½" x 6½".

With right sides together, make 6 pairs of Red and Ivory.

Follow the Half-Square Triangle instructions.

Center and trim each half-square triangle to 5½" x 5½".

Position the pieces following the diagram and sew 3 pinwheel blocks. Press.

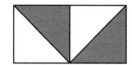

Pinwheel
Assemble 3

Pinwheel Stem & Leaves:

Cut 2 Green and 2 Gold strips 2½" x 27".

Cut 3 Brown stems 2½" x 8½".

Sew a section of Green-Gold-Gold-Green 27" wide strips together side by side to make a piece 8½" x 27". Press.

Cut the piece into 6 sections 4½" x 8½".

Sew a Green-Gold section to a Brown stem to another Green-Gold section to make a leaves/stem section. Press. Make 3.

Sew a Stem section to the bottom of each Pinwheel. Press.

Label 1 Pinwheel for Row 1 and set it aside.

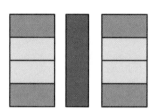

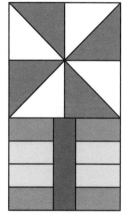

Stem & Leaves
Assemble 3

Pinwheel Block
Make 3

Pinwheel Blocks for Row 2:

Add the following pieces to the remaining Pinwheel Blocks for Row 2:

Cut 2 Green strips 2½" x 10½" for the top of each block.

Cut 4 Green strips 2½" x 20½" for the sides of each block.

Sew the top 10½" strips to 2 Pinwheels. Press.

Sew the side 20½" strips to 2 Pinwheels. Press.

Tops of Blocks for Row 2:

Cut 2 Brown strips 2½" x 14½" for the top of each block..

Cut 1 Blue strip 2½" x 10½" for the top of House 3 block.

Sew the Brown top strip to 2 Pinwheel blocks.

Sew the Blue top strip to House 3 block.

SASHINGS:

Cut the following 2½" x 38½" strips:

1 Blue for top,

1 Red for between Rows 1 & 2,

1 Gold for the bottom.

ASSEMBLY:

Arrange all Blocks on a work surface or table.

Refer to diagram for block placement and direction.

Sew blocks together in 2 rows, 3 blocks per row. Press.

Sew the Blue sashing to the top of Row 1. Press.

Sew the Red sashing to the top of Row 2. Press.

Sew the Gold sashing to the bottom of Row 2. Press.

Sew the rows together. Press.

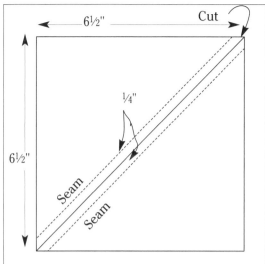

Half-Square Triangle Diagram
1. Place 2 squares right sides together.
2. Draw a diagonal line from corner to corner.
3. Stitch $\frac{1}{4}$" on each side of the line.
4. Cut squares apart on the diagonal line.
5. Open the 2 new squares with 2 colors.
6. Press. Trim off dog-ears.
7. Trim to $5\frac{1}{2}$" x $5\frac{1}{2}$".

Pieced Border #1:

Preparing the Pieces:
Sew 2 Green strips end to end to make a piece $52\frac{1}{2}$" long.
Sew 2 Ivory strips end to end to make a piece $52\frac{1}{2}$" long.
Sew the Green strip and the Ivory strip together side by side to make a piece $4\frac{1}{2}$" x $52\frac{1}{2}$".
Cut into 21 pieces $2\frac{1}{2}$" x $4\frac{1}{2}$".

Repeat for Blue and Ivory strips.

Cut 2 additional Ivory and 2 additional Blue squares $2\frac{1}{2}$" x $2\frac{1}{2}$".

Sewing the Strips:
Top Row:
Sew 9 Ivory-Green pieces to make a $2\frac{1}{2}$" wide strip.
Sew an Ivory square to the end. Press.
Bottom Row:
Sew 9 Ivory-Blue pieces to make a $2\frac{1}{2}$" wide strip.
Sew an Ivory square to the end. Press.
For each side:
Sew 6 Green-Ivory pieces to make a $2\frac{1}{2}$" wide strip.
Add 6 Blue-Ivory pieces.
Sew a Blue square to the bottom end. Press.

Sew the top and bottom rows to the quilt. Press.
Sew the sides to the quilt. Press.

Border #2:
Cut $1\frac{1}{2}$" strips.
Sew strips together end to end.
Cut 2 strips $1\frac{1}{2}$" x $50\frac{1}{2}$" for sides.
Cut 2 strips $1\frac{1}{2}$" x $44\frac{1}{2}$" for top and bottom.
Sew side borders to the quilt. Press.
Sew top and bottom borders to the quilt. Press.

Border #3:
Cut $4\frac{1}{2}$" strips.
Sew strips together end to end.
Cut 2 strips $4\frac{1}{2}$" x $52\frac{1}{2}$" for sides.
Cut 2 strips $4\frac{1}{2}$" x $52\frac{1}{2}$" for top and bottom.
Sew side borders to the quilt. Press.
Sew top and bottom borders to the quilt. Press.

FINISHING:
Quilting:
See Basic Instructions on pages 26 - 28.
Binding:
Cut six $2\frac{1}{2}$" strips.
Sew together end to end to equal 232".
See Binding Instructions on page 27.

Butterflies & Dragonflies
Dandelion Girl

photos on pages 6 - 7

SIZE: 49" x 58"

YARDAGE:

We used a *Moda* "Dandelion Girl" by Fig Tree
　'Jelly Roll' collection of 2½" fabric strips
　- we purchased 1 'Jelly Roll'

½ yard Apricot	OR	6 strips
½ yard Green	OR	5 strips
⅓ yard Yellow	OR	4 strips
¼ yard Aqua	OR	3 strips
⅞ yard Ivory	OR	12 strips
½ yard Brown	OR	6 strips

Border #1	Purchase ¼ yard Brown
Border #2 & Binding	Purchase 1⅛ yards Light Green
Backing	Purchase 2¾ yards
Batting	Purchase 57" x 66"

Sewing machine, needle, thread
DMC Brown Pearl Cotton or 6-ply Floss

PREPARATION FOR BLOCKS:

Apricot Pieced Squares:
　Cut 2 strips 2½" x 40".
　Sew the strips together side by side to make a piece 4½" x 40".
　Cut the piece into 10 squares 4" x 4".
　　Tip: Trim ¼" from each end of the 4½" side.

Yellow-Ivory Pieced Squares:
　Use 2½" wide strips.
　Cut 1 Yellow and 1 Ivory strip 2½" x 32".
　Sew the strips together side by side to make a piece 4½" x 32".
　Cut the piece into 8 squares 4" x 4".
　　Tip: Trim ¼" from each end of the 4½" side.

HALF-SQUARE TRIANGLES PREPARATION:

Apricot and Green Squares:
Sew leftover Apricot pieces end to end.
　Cut 2 Apricot strips 2½" x 45".
　Sew the strips together side by side to make a piece 4½" x 45".
　Cut into 10 squares 4½" x 4½".
Repeat for Green strips.

Aqua and Yellow Squares:
Cut 2 Aqua strips 2½" x 36".
　Sew the strips together side by side to make a piece 4½" x 36".
　Cut into 8 squares 4½" x 4½".
Repeat for Yellow strips.

HALF-SQUARE TRIANGLES:
　With right sides together match 10 pairs of Apricot and Green,
　　8 pairs of Aqua and Yellow.
　Follow the directions for Half-Square Triangles above.
　Make 20 Apricot-Green and 16 Aqua-Yellow half-square triangles.
　Center and trim all squares to 4" x 4".

Center Strips for Bodies:
　Cut 9 Brown strips 1" x 7½", one strip per block.
　Cut 5 Green strips 1" x 4", one strip for each Block A.
　Cut 4 Yellow strips 1" x 4", one strip for each Block B.

Block Borders:
　Cut 18 Brown strips 1¼" x 11" for sides.
　Cut 18 Brown strips 1¼" x 9½" for top and bottom.

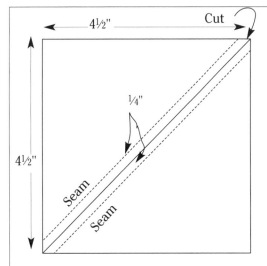

Half-Square Triangle Diagram
1. Place 2 squares right sides together.
2. Draw a diagonal line from corner to corner.
3. Stitch ¼" on each side of the line.
4. Cut squares apart on the diagonal line.
5. Open the 2 new squares with 2 colors.
6. Press. Trim off dog-ears.
7. Trim to 4" x 4".

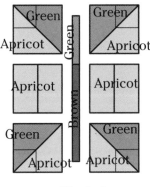

Block A
Pieces for
Butterfly

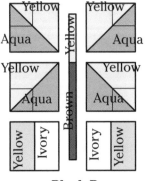

Block B
Pieces for
Dragonfly

SEW THE BLOCKS:
Follow the diagrams for
　Blocks A and B,
　paying attention to
　color placement and
　direction.

Sew the blocks together
　in columns. Press.

Sew the columns together to
　make the block.

Make 5 of Block A and
　4 of Block B.

Sew the side borders to
　each block. Press.

Sew the top and bottom
　borders to each
　block. Press.

SASHING:
Sew Ivory strips end to end.
  Cut 18 Ivory vertical sashings 2½" x 12½".
  Cut 6 Ivory top and bottom sashings 2½" x 39½".

ASSEMBLY:
  Arrange all blocks and sashings on a work surface or table.
  Refer to diagram for block placement and direction.
  Sew the vertical sashings and blocks to form each row. Press.
  Add the top and bottom sashings to each row. Press.
  Sew rows together. Press.

Embroider the
antennae with
Brown
pearl cotton.

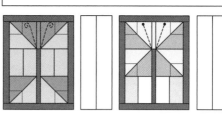

Row 1

| Block A | Block B | Block A |

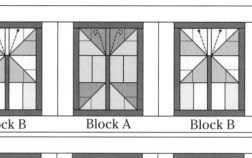

Row 2

| Block B | Block A | Block B |

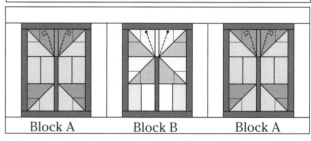

Row 3

| Block A | Block B | Block A |

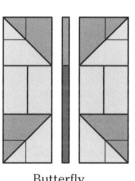

Butterfly
Block A
Assembly

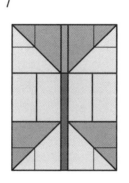

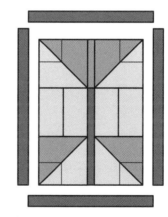

Butterfly - **Block A**
Make 5

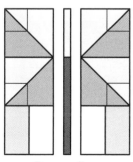

Dragonfly
Block B
Assembly

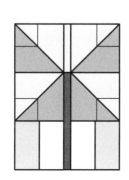

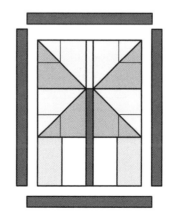

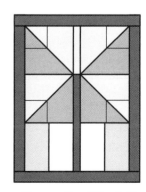

Dragonfly - **Block B**
Make 4

Strip Lovers 17

Butterflies & Dragonflies - Quilt Assembly Diagram

ADD THE BORDERS:

Border #1:

Cut 1½" wide strips.

Sew strips together end to end.

    Cut 2 strips 1½" x 48½" for sides.

    Cut 2 strips 1½" x 41½" for top and bottom.

    Sew side borders to the quilt. Press.

    Sew top and bottom borders to the quilt. Press.

Border #2:

Cut 4½" strips.

Sew strips together end to end.

    Cut 2 strips 4½" x 50½" for sides.

    Cut 2 strips 4½" x 49½" for top and bottom.

    Sew side borders to the quilt. Press.

    Sew top and bottom borders to the quilt. Press.

FINISHING:

Quilting: See Basic Instructions on pages 26 - 28.

Binding: Cut six 2½" strips.

    Sew together end to end to equal 222".

    See Binding Instructions on page 27.

Garden Inspirations

photos on pages 8 - 9

SIZE: 66" x 70"

YARDAGE:
We used a *Moda* "Garden Inspirations" by Kansas Troubles Quilters
'Jelly Roll' collection of 2½" fabric strips
- we purchased 1 'Jelly Roll'

½ yard Navy	OR	5 strips
⅞ yard Tan	OR	11 strips
⅓ yard Burgundy	OR	4 strips
⅓ yard Purple	OR	4 strips
½ yard Green	OR	6 strips
½ yard Black	OR	5 strips
⅓ yard Golden Brown	OR	4 strips

Border #1	Purchase ⅜ yard Green
Border #2	Purchase ½ yard Golden Brown
Border #3 & Binding	Purchase 1⅝ yards Burgundy
Backing	Purchase 4 yards
Batting	Purchase 74" x 78"

Sewing machine, needle, thread

PREPARATION FOR BLOCKS

Corner Squares:
You will need 8 Green and 4 Golden Brown.
Sew 4 Green strips end to end.
> Cut 3 Green strips 48" long.
> Sew the strips together side by side to make a piece 6½" x 48".
> Cut the piece into 8 sections 6" long".
> Center and trim each section to 6" x 6".
> Label 4 for Block #2 and 4 for Block #3.

Cut 3 Golden Brown strips 24" long.
> Sew the strips together side by side to make a piece 6½" x 24".
> Cut the piece into 4 sections 6" long.
> Center and trim each section to 6" x 6".
> Label these squares for Block #4.
NOTE: Any leftover Golden Brown strips will be used as Tan.

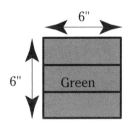
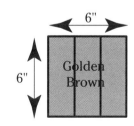

Corner Squares

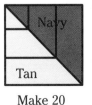
Make 20

Make 16

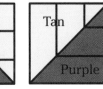
Make 16

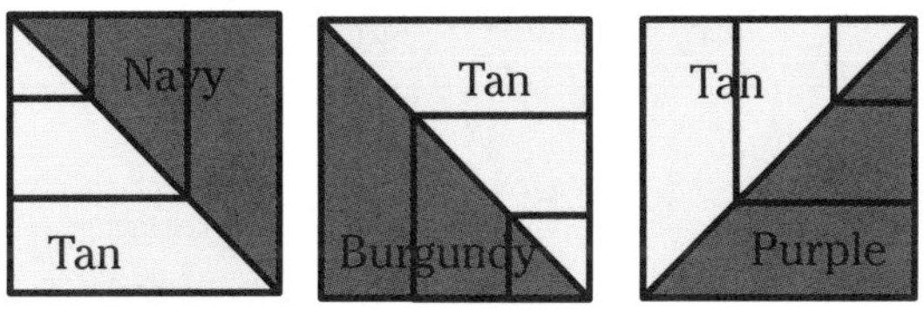

Label the Squares:
Big Block 1:
12 Navy-Tan
4 Burgundy-Tan
Big Block 2:
8 Burgundy-Tan
4 Purple-Tan
Big Block 3:
4 Burgundy-Tan
8 Purple-Tan
Big Block 4:
8 Navy-Tan
4 Burgundy-Tan

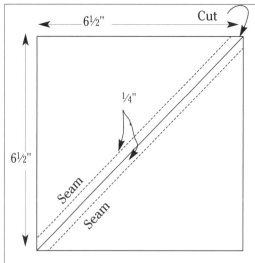

Half-Square Triangle Diagram
1. Place 2 squares right sides together.
2. Draw a diagonal line from corner to corner.
3. Stitch ¼" on each side of the line.
4. Cut squares apart on the diagonal line.
5. Open the 2 new squares with 2 colors.
6. Press. Trim off dog-ears.
7. Trim to 6" x 6".

HALF-SQUARE TRIANGLES:
Tan Squares - Make 26:
> Sew 13 Tan strips end to end. Cut 3 strips 169" long.
> Sew the strips together side by side to make a piece 6½" x 169".
> Cut this piece into 26 squares 6½" x 6½".

Navy Squares - Make 10:
> Sew 5 Navy strips end to end. Cut 3 strips 65" long.
> Sew the strips together side by side to make a piece 6½" x 65".
> Cut this piece into 10 squares 6½" x 6½".

Purple Squares - Make 8:
> Sew 4 Purple strips end to end. Cut 3 strips 52" long.
> Sew the strips together side by side to make a piece 6½" x 52".
> Cut this piece into 8 squares 6½" x 6½".

Burgundy Squares - Make 8:
> Sew 4 Burgundy strips end to end. Cut 3 strips 52" long.
> Sew the strips together side by side to make a piece 6½" x 52".
> Cut this piece into 8 squares 6½" x 6½".

With right sides together make the following pairs:
> 10 Navy-Tan   8 Burgundy-Tan   8 Purple-Tan
Follow the instructions for Half-Square Triangles to make:
> 20 Navy-Tan   16 Burgundy-Tan   16 Purple-Tan
Center and trim all squares to 6" x 6".

SEW THE BLOCKS:
Following the diagrams, arrange the half-square triangles as shown and sew the blocks together. Press.
Arrange the blocks as shown.
Sew 2 rows of 2 blocks each. Press.
Sew the rows together. Press.

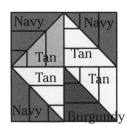

Block A
Make 4

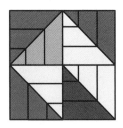

Turn the block 90°
for each corner.

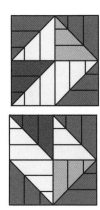

Big Block 1

**You'll need these Squares for
Big Block 1:**
12 Navy-Tan
4 Burgundy-Tan

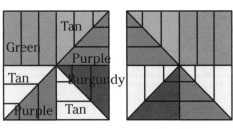

Block B
Make 4

Turn the block 90°
for each corner.

**You'll need these Squares for
Big Block 2:**
4 Burgundy-Tan
8 Purple-Tan
4 Green Corners

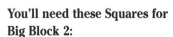

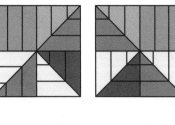

Big Block 2

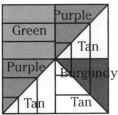
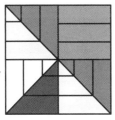

Block C
Make 4

Turn the block 90°
for each corner.

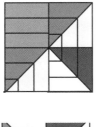
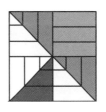

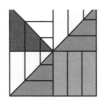

Big Block 3

**You'll need these Squares for
Big Block 3:**
4 Burgundy-Tan
8 Purple Tan
4 Green Corners

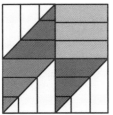

Block D
Make 4

Turn the block 90°
for each corner.

Big Block 4

**You'll need these Squares for
Big Block 4:**
8 Navy-Tan
4 Burgundy-Tan
4 Golden Brown Corners

ADD SASHINGS:

For Big Block 1:
> Cut 4 Green strips 2½" x 11½" and 2 Black strips 2½" x 13½".
> Sew 2 Green strips end to end for each side. Press.
> Sew the Black strips end to end for the bottom. Press.
> Sew the Green side strips to the block. Press.
> Sew the Black strip to the bottom of the block. Press.

For Big Block 2:
> Cut 2½" wide Black strips: 24½", 22½", 13½", 11½".
> Sew the 22½" strip to the right side of the block. Press.
> Sew the 11½" & 13½" strips end to end and then to the top of
>   the block. Press.
> Sew the 24½" strip to the left side of the block. Press.

For Big Block 3:
> Cut 2½" wide Black strips: two 22½", two 13½".
> Sew the 22½" strips to the sides of the block. Press.
> Sew the 13½" strips end to end and then to the bottom of
>   the block. Press.

For Big Block 4:
> Cut 4 Green strips 2½" x 11½" and 2 Black strips 2½" x 13½".
> Sew 2 Green strips end to end for each side. Press.
> Sew the Black strips end to end for the bottom. Press.
> Sew the Green side strips to the block. Press.
> Sew the Black strip to the top of the block. Press.

Big Block 1

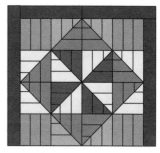
Big Block 2

Big Block 3

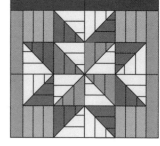
Big Block 4

ASSEMBLY - SEW BLOCKS TOGETHER:
> Arrange all Blocks on a work surface or table.
> Refer to diagram for block placement and direction.
> Sew blocks together in 2 rows, 2 blocks per row. Press.
> Sew rows together. Press.

Garden Inspirations
Quilt Assembly Diagram

Top & Bottom Border #1:
Cut 4½" strips.
Sew strips together end to end.
    Cut 2 strips 4½" x 52½" for top and bottom.
    Sew top and bottom borders to the quilt. Press.

Border #2:
Cut 2½" strips.
Sew strips together end to end.
    Cut 2 strips 2½" x 56½" for sides.
    Cut 2 strips 2½" x 56½" for top and bottom.
    Sew side borders to the quilt. Press.
    Sew top and bottom borders to the quilt. Press.

Border #3:
Cut 5½" strips. Sew strips together end to end.
    Cut 2 strips 5½" x 60½" for sides.
    Cut 2 strips 5½" x 66½" for top and bottom.
    Sew side borders to the quilt. Press.
    Sew top and bottom borders to the quilt. Press.

FINISHING:

Quilting:

    See Basic Instructions on pages 26 - 28.

Binding:

    Cut seven 2½" strips.
    Sew together end to end to equal 280".
    See Binding Instructions on page 27.

Tips for Working with Strips

TIPS: As a Guide for Yardage:

Each $1/4$ yard or a 'Fat Quarter' equals 3 strips

A pre-cut 'Jelly Roll' strip is $2^{1}/_{2}$" x 44"

Cut 'Fat Quarter' strips to $2^{1}/_{2}$" x 22"

Pre-cut strips are cut on the crosswise grain and are prone to stretching. These tips will help reduce stretching and make your quilt lay flat for quilting.

1. If you are cutting yardage, cut on the grain. Cut fat quarters on grain, parallel to the 18" side.

2. When sewing crosswise grain strips together, take care not to stretch the strips. If you detect any puckering as you go, rip out the seam and sew it again.

3. Press, Do Not Iron. Carefully open fabric, with the seam to one side, press without moving the iron. A back-and-forth ironing motion stretches the fabric.

4. Reduce the wiggle in your borders with this technique from garment making. First, accurately cut your borders to the exact measure of the quilt top. Then, before sewing the border to the quilt, run a double row of stay stitches along the outside edge to maintain the original shape and prevent stretching. Pin the border to the quilt, taking care not to stretch the quilt top to make it fit. Pinning reduces slipping and stretching.

Rotary Cutting Tips

Rotary Cutter: Friend or Foe

A rotary cutter is a wonderful and useful. When not used correctly, the sharp blade can be a dangerous tool. Follow these safety tips:

1. Never cut toward you.

2. Use a sharp blade. Pressing harder on a dull blade can cause the blade to jump the ruler and injure your fingers.

3. Always disengage the blade before the cutter leaves your hand, even if you intend to pick it up immediately.

Rotary cutters have been caught when lifting fabric, have fallen onto the floor and have cut fingers.

Basic Cutting Instructions

Tips for Accurate Cutting:

Accurate cutting is easy when using a rotary cutter with a sharp blade, a cutting mat, and a transparent ruler. Begin by pressing your fabric and then follow these steps:

1. Folding:

a) Fold the fabric with the selvage edges together. Smooth the fabric flat. If needed, fold again to make your fabric length smaller than the length of the ruler.

b) Align the fold with one of the guide lines on the mat. This is important to avoid getting a kink in your strip.

2. Cutting:

a) Align the ruler with a guide line on the mat. Press down on the ruler to prevent it shifting or have someone help hold the ruler. Hold the rotary cutter along the edge of the ruler and cut off the selvage edge.

b) Also using the guide line on the mat, cut the ends straight.

c) Strips for making the quilt top may be cut on 'crosswise grain' (from selvage to selvage) or 'on grain' (parallel to the selvage edge).

Strips for borders should be cut on grain (parallel to the selvage edge) to prevent wavy edges and make quilting easier.

d) When cutting strips, move the ruler, NOT the fabric.

Basic Sewing Instructions

You now have precisely cut strips that are exactly the correct width. You are well on your way to blocks that fit together perfectly. Accurate sewing is the next important step.

Matching Edges:

1. Carefully line up the edges of your strips. Many times, if the underside is off a little, your seam will be off by ⅛". This does not sound like much until you have 8 seams in a block, each off by ⅛". Now your finished block is a whole inch wrong!

2. Pin the pieces together to prevent them shifting.

Seam Allowance:

I cannot stress enough the importance of accurate ¼" seams. All the quilts in this book are measured for ¼" seams unless otherwise indicated.

Most sewing machine manufacturers offer a Quarter-inch foot. A Quarter-inch foot is the most worthwhile investment you can make in your quilting.

Pressing:

I want to talk about pressing even before we get to sewing because proper pressing can make the difference between a quilt that wins a ribbon at the quilt show and one that does not.

Press, do NOT iron. What does that mean? Many of us want to move the iron back and forth along the seam. This "ironing" stretches the strip out of shape and creates errors that accumulate as the quilt is constructed. Believe it or not, there is a correct way to press your seams, and here it is:

1. Do NOT use steam with your iron. If you need a little water, spritz it on.

2. Place your fabric flat on the ironing board without opening the seam. Set a hot iron on the seam and count to 3. Lift the iron and move to the next position along the seam. Repeat until the entire seam is pressed. This sets and sinks the threads into the fabric.

3. Now, carefully lift the top strip and fold it away from you so the seam is on one side. Usually the seam is pressed toward the darker fabric, but often the direction of the seam is determined by the piecing requirements.

4. Press the seam open with your fingers. Add a little water or spray starch if it wants to close again. Lift the iron and place it on the seam. Count to 3. Lift the iron again and continue until the seam is pressed. Do NOT use the tip of the iron to push the seam open. So many people do this and wonder later why their blocks are not fitting together.

5. Most critical of all: For accuracy every seam must be pressed before the next seam is sewn.

Working with 'Crosswise Grain' strips:

Strips cut on the crosswise grain (from selvage to selvage) have problems similar to bias edges and are prone to stretching. To reduce stretching and make your quilt lay flat for quilting, keep these tips in mind.

1. Take care not to stretch the strips as you sew.

2. Adjust the sewing thread tension and the presser foot pressure if needed.

3. If you detect any puckering as you go, rip out the seam and sew it again. It is much easier to take out a seam now than to do it after the block is sewn.

Sewing Bias Edges:

Bias edges wiggle and stretch out of shape very easily. They are not recommended for beginners, but even a novice can accomplish bias edges if these techniques are employed.

1. Stabilize the bias edge with one of these methods:

    a) Press with spray starch.

    b) Press freezer paper or removable iron-on stabilizer to the back of the fabric.

    c) Sew a double row of stay stitches along the bias edge and ⅛" from the bias edge. This is a favorite technique of garment makers.

2. Pin, pin, pin! I know many of us dislike pinning, but when working with bias edges, pinning makes the difference between intersections that match and those that do not.

Building Better Borders:

Wiggly borders make a quilt very difficult to finish. However, wiggly borders can be avoided with these techniques.

1. Cut the borders on grain. That means cutting your strips parallel to the selvage edge.

2. Accurately cut your borders to the exact measure of the quilt.

3. If your borders are piece stripped from crosswise grain fabrics, press well with spray starch and sew a double row of stay stitches along the outside edge to maintain the original shape and prevent stretching.

4. Pin the border to the quilt, taking care not to stretch the quilt top to make it fit. Pinning reduces slipping and stretching.

Applique Instructions

Basic Turned Edge:

1. Trace pattern onto template plastic.

2. Cut out the shape leaving a scant ¼" fabric border all around and clip the curves.

3. Place the template plastic on the wrong side of the fabric. Spray edges with starch.

4. Press the ⅛" border over the edge of the template plastic with the tip of a hot iron. Press firmly.

5. Remove the template, maintaining the folded edge on the back of the fabric.

6. Position the shape on the quilt and Blindstitch in place.

Basic Needle Turn:

1. Cut out the shape leaving a ¼" fabric border all around.

2. Baste the shapes to the quilt, keeping the basting stitches away from the edge of the fabric.

3. Begin with all areas that are under other layers and work to the topmost layer.

4. For an area no more than 2" ahead of where you are working, trim to ⅛" and clip the curves.

5. Using the needle, roll the edge under and sew tiny Blindstitches to secure.

Using Fusible Web for Iron-on Applique:

1. Trace the pattern onto *Steam a Seam 2* fusible web.

2. Press the patterns onto the wrong side of the fabric.

3. Cut out patterns exactly on the drawn line.

4. Score the web paper with a pin, then remove the paper.

5. Position the fabric, fusible side down, on the quilt. Press with a hot iron following the fusible web manufacturer's instructions.

6. Stitch around the edge by hand.

Optional: Stabilize the wrong side of the fabric with your favorite stabilizer.

Use a size 80 machine embroidery needle. Fill the bobbin with lightweight basting thread and thread the machine with a machine embroidery thread that complements the color being appliqued.

Set your machine for a Zigzag stitch and adjust the thread tension if needed. Use a scrap to experiment with different stitch widths and lengths until you find the one you like best.

Sew slowly.

Basic Layering Instructions

Marking Your Quilt:

If you choose to mark your quilt for hand or machine quilting, it is much easier to do so before layering. Press your quilt before you begin. Here are some handy tips regarding marking.

1. A disappearing pen may vanish before you finish.

2. Use a White pencil on dark fabrics.

3. If using a washable Blue pen, remember that pressing may make the pen permanent.

Pieced Backings:

1. Press the backing fabric before measuring.

2. If possible cut backing fabrics on grain, parallel to the selvage edges.

3. Piece 3 parts rather than 2 whenever possible, sewing 2 side borders to the center. This reduces stress on the pieced seam.

4. The backing and batting should extend at least 2" on each side of the quilt.

Creating a Quilt Sandwich:

1. Press the backing and top to remove all wrinkles.

2. Lay the backing wrong side up on the table.

3. Position the batting over the backing and smooth out all wrinkles.

4. Center the quilt top over the batting leaving a 2" border all around.

5. Pin the layers together with 2" safety pins positioned a handwidth apart. A grapefruit spoon makes inserting the pins easier. Leaving the pins open in the container speeds up the basting on the next quilt.

Basic Quilting Instructions

Hand Quilting:

Many quilters enjoy the serenity of hand quilting. Because the quilt is handled a great deal, it is important to securely baste the sandwich together. Place the quilt in a hoop and don't forget to hide your knots.

Machine Quilting:

All the quilts in this book were machine quilted. Some were quilted on a large, free-arm quilting machine and others were quilted on a sewing machine. If you have never machine quilted before, practice on some scraps first.

Straight Line Machine Quilting Tips:

1. Pin baste the layers securely.

2. Set up your sewing machine with a size 80 quilting needle and a walking foot.

3. Experimenting with the decorative stitches on your machine adds interest to your quilt. You do not have to quilt the entire piece with the same stitch. Variety is the spice of life, so have fun trying out stitches you have never used before as well as your favorite stand-bys.

Free Motion Machine Quilting Tips:

1. Pin baste the layers securely.

2. Set up your sewing machine with a spring needle, a quilting foot, and lower the feed dogs.

Basic Mitered Binding
Instructions

A Perfect Finish:

The binding endures the most stress on a quilt and is usually the first thing to wear out. For this reason, we recommend using a double fold binding.

1. Trim the backing and batting even with the quilt edge.

2. If possible cut strips on the crosswise grain because a little bias in the binding is a Good thing. This is the only place in the quilt where bias is helpful, for it allows the binding to give as it is turned to the back and sewn in place.

3. Strips are usually cut 2½" wide, but check the instructions for your project before cutting.

4. Sew strips end to end to make a long strip sufficient to go all around the quilt plus 4"- 6".

5. With wrong sides together, fold the strip in half lengthwise. Press.

6. Stretch out your hand and place your little finger at the corner of the quilt top. Place the binding where your thumb touches the edge of the quilt. Aligning the edge of the quilt with the raw edges of the binding, pin the binding in place along the first side.

7. Leaving a 2" tail for later use, begin sewing the binding to the quilt with a ¼" seam.

For Mitered Corners:

1. Stop ¼" from the first corner. Leave the needle in the quilt and turn it 90°. Hit the reverse button on your machine and back off the quilt leaving the threads connected.

2. Fold the binding perpendicular to the side you sewed, making a 45° angle. Carefully maintaining the first fold, bring the binding back along the edge to be sewn.

3. Carefully align the edges of the binding with the quilt edge and sew as you did the first side. Repeat this process until you reach the tail left at the beginning. Fold the tail out of the way and sew until you are ¼" from the beginning stitches.

4. Remove the quilt from the machine. Fold the quilt out of the way and match the binding tails together. Carefully sew the binding tails with a ¼" seam. You can do this by hand if you prefer.

Finishing the Binding:

5. Trim the seam to reduce bulk.

6. Finish stitching the binding to the quilt across the join you just sewed.

7. Turn the binding to the back of the quilt. To reduce bulk at the corners, fold the miter in the opposite direction from which it was folded on the front.

8. Hand-sew a Blind stitch on the back of the quilt to secure the binding in place.

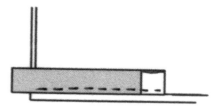

Align the raw edge of the binding with the raw edge of the quilt top. Start about 8" from the corner and go along the first side with a ¼" seam.

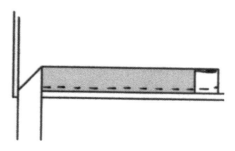

Stop ¼" from the edge. Then stitch a slant to the corner (through both layers of binding)... lift up, then down, as you line up the edge. Fold the binding back.

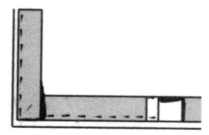

Align the raw edge again. Continue stitching the next side with a ¼" seam as you sew the binding in place.

Strawberry Lemonade

photo on pages 44 - 45

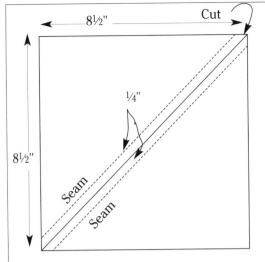

Half-Square Triangle Diagram
1. Place 2 squares right sides together.
2. Draw a diagonal line from corner to corner.
3. Stitch ¼" on each side of the line.
4. Cut squares apart on the diagonal line.
5. Open the 2 new squares with 2 colors.
6. Press. Trim off dog-ears.
7. Trim to 8" x 8".

SIZE: 55" x 63"

YARDAGE:
We used a *Moda* "Strawberry Lemonade" by Me & My Sister
'Jelly Roll' collection of 2½" fabric strips
- we purchased 1 'Jelly Roll'

⅝ yard White	OR	8 strips
½ yard Pink	OR	6 strips
½ yard Yellow	OR	7 strips
½ yard Green	OR	6 strips
½ yard Blue	OR	6 strips
¼ yard Med White	OR	3 strips

Border #1	Purchase ¼ yard Green
Border #2 & Binding	Purchase 1⅙ yards Pink
Backing	Purchase 3⅙ yards
Batting	Purchase 63" x 71"

Sewing machine, needle, thread

PREPARATION FOR BLOCKS
Sew 8 White strips end to end. Cut 4 strips 76½" long.
Sew the strips together side by side to make a piece 8½" x 76½". Press.
Cut the piece into 9 squares 8½" x 8½".
Sew the 3 Medium White strips end to end. Cut 4 strips 25½" long.
Sew the strips together side by side to make a piece 8½" x 25½". Press.
Cut the piece into 3 squares 8½" x 8½".
For all other colors, sew 5 strips end to end. Cut 4 strips 51" long.
Sew the strips together side by side to make a piece 8½" x 51".
Cut the piece into 6 squares 8½" x 8½".
You will need the following squares: 6 Pink, 6 Yellow, 6 Green, 6 Blue, 3 Medium White, 9 White.

HALF-SQUARE TRIANGLES
Pair the following blocks and place them right sides together:
3 White-Pink, 3 Pink-Yellow, 3 Yellow-Green, 3 Green-Blue, 3 Blue-White, 3 White-Medium White.
Follow the instructions for making Half-Square Triangles.
Trim all blocks to 8" x 8".

ASSEMBLY:
Arrange all Blocks on a work surface or table.
Refer to diagram for block placement and direction.
Sew blocks together in 6 rows, 6 blocks per row. Press.
Sew rows together. Press.

Top Row Piano Keys:
Cut 1 Pink, 1 Yellow and 1 Green strips 2½" x 36".
Arrange the strips Yellow-Pink-Green and sew them together side by side. Press.
Cut 8 strips 4½" x 6½".
Sew the strips together. Press.
Center and trim to 4½" x 45½" and sew to the top of the quilt. Press.

Bottom Row Piano Keys:
Cut 2 Pink, 2 Blue and 2 Yellow strips 2½" x 16".
Arrange the strips Yellow-Blue-Yellow and Pink-Blue-Pink.
Sew the strips together. Press.
Cut each set into 4 strips 4½" x 6½".
Sew the strips together alternating the sets. Press.
Center and trim to 4½" x 45½" and sew to the bottom of the quilt. Press.

continued on page 30

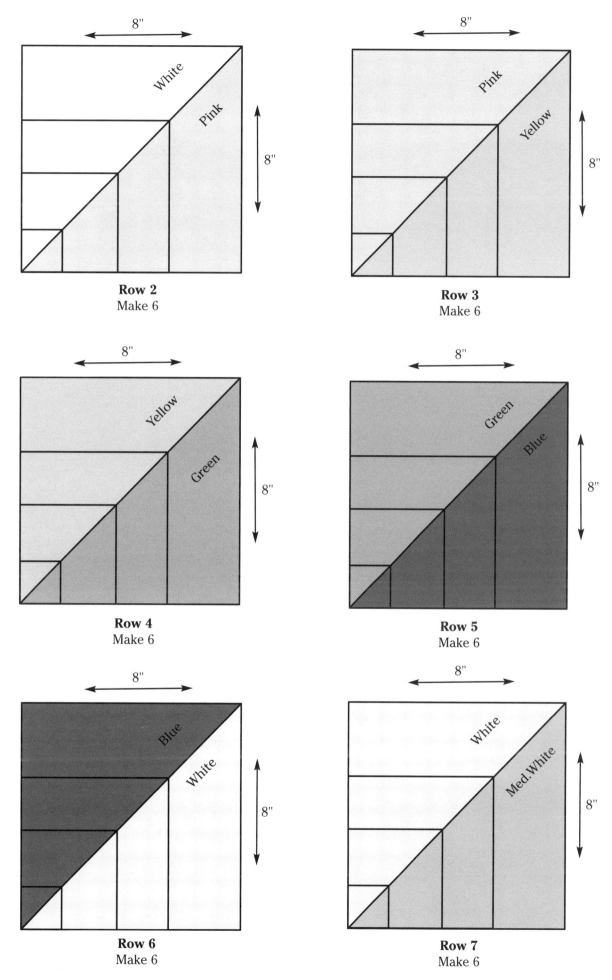

Row 2
Make 6

Row 3
Make 6

Row 4
Make 6

Row 5
Make 6

Row 6
Make 6

Row 7
Make 6

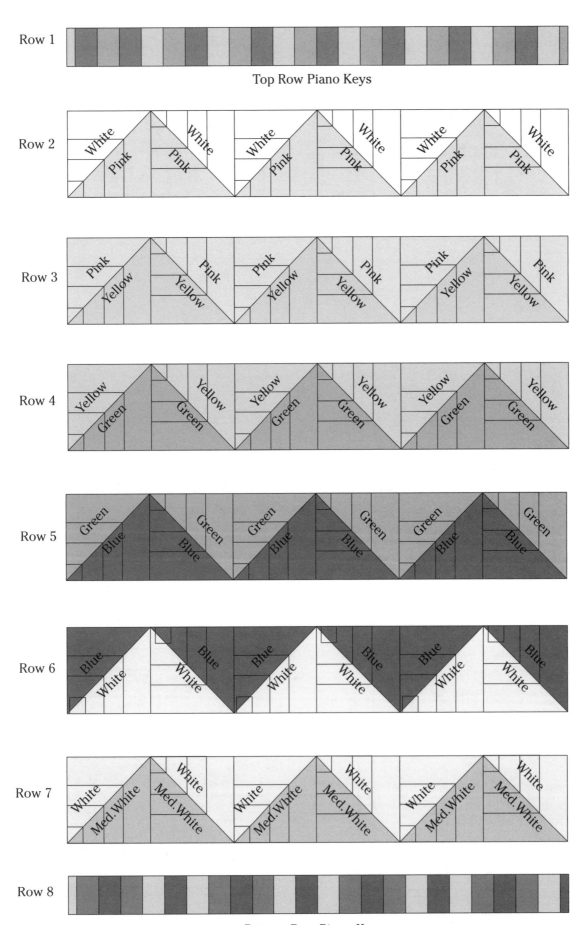

Row 1

Top Row Piano Keys

Row 2

Row 3

Row 4

Row 5

Row 6

Row 7

Row 8

Bottom Row Piano Keys

Strawberry Lemonade - Quilt Assembly Diagram

Border #1:
Cut 1½" strips.
Sew strips together end to end.
    Cut 2 strips 1½" x 53½" for sides.
    Cut 2 strips 1½" x 47½" for top and bottom.
    Sew side borders to the quilt. Press.
    Sew top and bottom borders to the quilt. Press.

Border #2:
Cut 4½" strips.
Sew strips together end to end.
    Cut 2 strips 4½" x 55½" for sides.
    Cut 2 strips 4½" x 55½" for top and bottom.
    Sew side borders to the quilt. Press.
    Sew top and bottom borders to the quilt. Press.

FINISHING:
Quilting: See Basic Instructions on pages 24 - 27.
Binding: Cut six 2½" strips.
    Sew together end to end to equal 244".
    See Binding Instructions on page 27.

Maypole

photo on pages 46 - 47

SIZE: 48" x 58"

YARDAGE:

We used a *Moda* "Maypole" by April Cornell
  'Jelly Roll' collection of 2½" fabric strips
  - we purchased 1 'Jelly Roll'

¾ yard Yellow	OR	10 strips
½ yard Purple	OR	6 strips
½ yard Green	OR	7 strips
⅙ yard Red	OR	2 strips
⅓ yard Light Blue	OR	4 strips
⅔ yard Dark Blue	OR	9 strips

Border #1   Purchase ¼ yard Red
Border #2 & Binding   Purchase 1⅙ yards Light Blue
Backing   Purchase 1⅝ yards
Batting   Purchase 56" x 66"
Sewing machine, needle, thread
Optional: 5 Blue 1¼" buttons

PREPARATION FOR BLOCKS

Yellow-Purple Half Square Triangles - Make 3
Yellow-Red Half Square Triangles - Make 1
Yellow-Light Green Half Square Triangles - Make 1

Sew 5 Yellow strips end to end.
  Cut 3 pieces 65" long.
  Sew the strips together side by side to make a piece 6½" x 65".
Cut 3 Purple strips 39" long.
  Sew together side by side to make 6½" x 39".
Cut 3 Red strips 13" long.
  Sew the strips together side by side to make a piece 6½" x 13".
Cut 3 Light Green strips 13" long.
  Sew the strips together side by side to make a piece 6½" x 13".

MAKE HALF-SQUARE TRIANGLES

Cut all pieces into squares 6½" x 6½".
With right sides together, make 10 pairs:
  6 Yellow-Purple, 2 Yellow-Red, and 2 Yellow-Light Green.
Follow the Half-Square Triangle instructions to make:
  12 Yellow-Purple, 4 Yellow-Red, and 4 Yellow-Light Green
  half-square triangles.
Trim all half-square triangles to 5½" x 5½".

Purple-Yellow
Half-Square
Triangles
Make 12

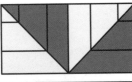

Block A
Pinwheel Assembly

Block A - Make 3
Use 2 for Row 1
Use 1 for Row 2

Block A for Row 1
Make 2

Follow the diagrams to assemble:
  3 Yellow-Purple "Block A" Pinwheels, 1 Yellow-Red "Block B" , and 1 Yellow-Green "Block C".

SEW BLOCKS A and B:

Row 1 - Blocks A:
  Set aside 1 Block A for Row 2.
  Cut 4 Dark Blue strips 2½" x 10½" for the sides.
  Cut 2 Dark Blue and 2 Light Blue strip 2½" x 14½" for the bottoms.
  Sew side strips to 2 Yellow-Purple Pinwheel A's. Press.
  Sew a Blue and Light Blue strip to the bottom of each block. Press.

Red-Yellow
Half-Square
Triangles
Make 4

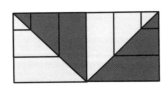
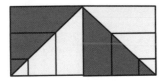

Block B
Pinwheel Assembly

Block B
Use 1 for Row 1

Block B for Row 1
Make 1

Row 1 - Block B:
  Cut 2 Dark Blue strips 2½" x 10½" for the top.
  Sew both Blue strips to the top of Yellow-Red Pinwheel B. Press.

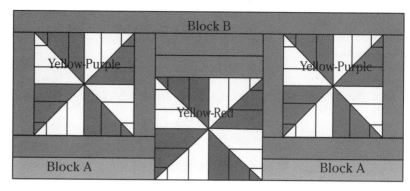

Assemble Row 1

ASSEMBLE ROW 1:
Row 1 - Sew Sections Together:
Sew the 3 blocks together, A-B-A to complete Row 1.
Press.

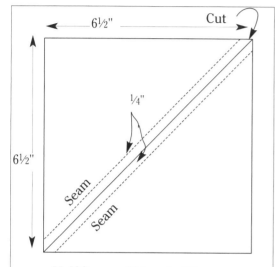

Half-Square Triangle Diagram
1. Place 2 squares right sides together.
2. Draw a diagonal line from corner to corner.
3. Stitch ¼" on each side of the line.
4. Cut squares apart on the diagonal line.
5. Open the 2 new squares with 2 colors.
6. Press. Trim off dog-ears.
7. Trim to 5½" x 5½".

Lt Green-Yellow Half-Square Triangles Make 4

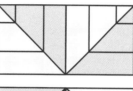
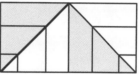

Block C Pinwheel Assembly

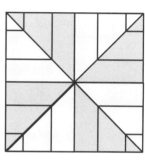

Block C for Row 2 Make 1

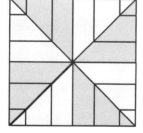

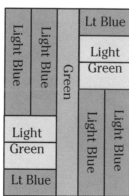

Block C Assembly

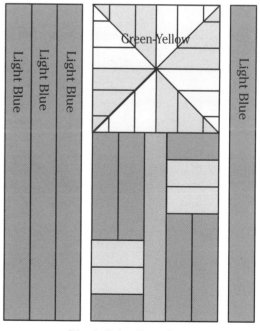

Block C for Row 2

SEW BLOCK C:

Row 2 - Block C:
Cut 4 Light Blue strips 2½" x 8½".
Cut 2 Light Blue strips 2½" x 4½".
Cut 4 Lighter Green strips 2½" x 4½" for leaves.
Cut 1 Bright Green strip 2½" x 14½" for stem.

Arrange the pieces following the Block C Assembly Diagram and sew the pieces together. Press.
Cut 4 Light Blue strips 2½" x 24½" for the sides.
Sew 3 strips to the left side of the block and 1 strip to the right side. Press.

continued on page 34

Maypole - continued from page 33

Row 2 - Block D:
Cut 4 Light Blue strips 2½" x 8½".
Cut 2 Light Blue strips 2½" x 4½".
Cut 4 Lighter Green strips 2½" x 4½" for leaves.
Cut 1 Bright Green strip 2½" x 14½" for the stem.
Arrange the pieces following the Block D Assembly
    Diagram and sew the pieces together. Press.
Cut 4 Light Blue strips 2½" x 24½" for the sides.
Sew 1 strip to the left side of the block and 3 strips to
    the right side. Press.

ASSEMBLE ROW 2:
Row 2 - Top Sashing and Center Stem:
Cut 1 Bright Green 2½" x 26½" strip for the long stem.
Cut 2 Blue strips 2½" x 18½" for the top.
Sew a Blue strip to the top of Block C and Block D.
Sew long Green stem between Block C and Block D

Row 2 - Bottom Sashing:
Cut 2 Green 2½" x 38½" strips for the grass.
Cut 2 Green 2½" x 10½" strips for the grass.
Cut 2 Green 2½" x 6½" strips for the grass.
Cut 3 Bright Green 2½" x 2½" squares for stem bottoms.
Sew the following strips end to end:
    Green 10½", Green 2½",
    Green 6½", Green 2½",
    Green 6½", Green 2½",
    Green 10½" to measure 38½". Press.
Sew this strip to the 2 Green 38½" pieces. Press.
Sew the 3-strip Green 38½" section to the bottom.
    Press.

ASSEMBLY:
Arrange Blocks and Rows on a work surface or table.
Refer to diagram.
Sew Row 1 to Row 2.

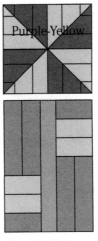

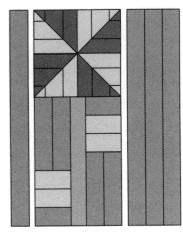

Purple-Yellow
Pinwheel A for Row 2

Block D - Assembly for Row 2

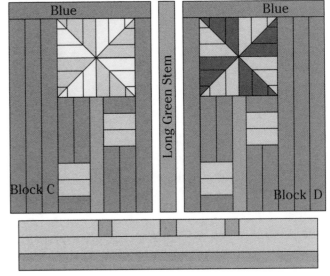

Row 2 Assembly

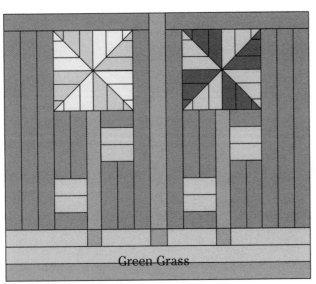

Assemble Row 2

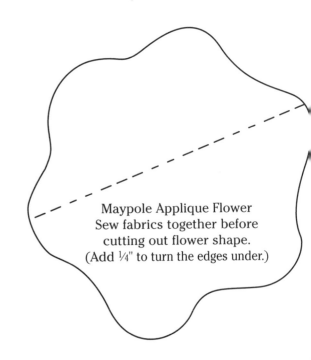

Maypole Applique Flower
Sew fabrics together before
cutting out flower shape.
(Add ¼" to turn the edges under.)

Maypole - Quilt Assembly Diagram

Border #1:
  Cut 1½" strips.
  Sew strips together end to end.
  Cut 2 strips 1½" x 48½" for sides.
  Cut 2 strips 1½" x 40½" for top and bottom.
  Sew side borders to the quilt. Press.
  Sew top and bottom borders to the quilt. Press.

Border #2:
  Cut 4½" strips.
  Sew strips together end to end.
  Cut 2 strips 4½" x 50½" for sides.
  Cut 2 strips 4½" x 48½" for top and bottom.
  Sew side borders to the quilt. Press.
  Sew top and bottom borders to the quilt. Press.

Optional Applique:
  Cut 2 Red strips 2½" x 18".
  Sew strips together to make a piece 4½" x 18".
  The applique pattern is on page 34.
  Trace and cut out 5 flowers.
  Follow the Basic Instructions for Applique on page 26.

FINISHING:
Quilting: See Basic Instructions on pages 24 - 27.
Binding: Cut five 2½" strips.
  Sew together end to end to equal 220".
  See Binding Instructions on page 27.
Buttons: Sew a button to each flower center after quilting.

Natural Garden

photo on pages 48 - 49

SIZE: 56" x 64"
YARDAGE:
We used a *Moda* "Natural Garden" by Holly Taylor
    'Jelly Roll' collection of 2½" fabric strips
    - we purchased 1 'Jelly Roll'

⅝ yard Ivory	OR	9 strips
⅜ yard Red	OR	5 strips
⅓ yard Lt Green	OR	4 strips
¼ yard Dk Green	OR	3 strips
½ yard Tan	OR	5 strips
⅓ yard Purple	OR	4 strips
⅓ yard Lavender	OR	4 strips

Border #4   Purchase ¼ yard Dark Green
Border #5   Purchase ¾ yards Ivory
Binding   Purchase ½ yard Lavender
Backing   Purchase 3¼ yards
Batting   Purchase 64" x 72"
Sewing machine, needle, thread

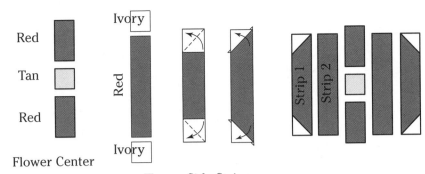

Flower Center

Flower Side Strips

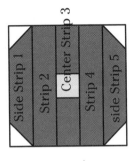

Assembled Flower

PREPARATION FOR BLOCKS

Flowers:
    Cut 12 Red strips 2½" x 10½" and 6 Red strips
        2½" x 4½".
    Cut 12 Ivory squares 2½" x 2½".
    Cut 3 Tan squares 2½" x 2½".

Flower Centers:
    Sew a 4½" strip to each side of the Tan
        squares for the center. Press.

Flower Side Strips:
    Position an Ivory square on each end of
        6 Red strips as shown.
    Sew on the diagonal as shown, fold back the
        flap to make a triangle on each end of strip.

Assemble Flowers:
    Position strips for each flower as shown in the
        diagram.
    Sew the 5 strips together. Press.

Stem and Leaf Sections:

Stems: Cut 2 Light Green strips 2½" x 20½" and 1 strip
        2½" x 12½".

Leaves:
    Sew remaining Light Green strips end to end.
    Cut 2 Green strips 2½" x 45" for leaves.
    Sew the 2 Green strips together side by side to make a
        piece 4½" x 45". Press.
    Cut the piece into 10 squares 4½" x 4½".

Background:

Leaves - Triple:
Cut 3 Ivory strips 2½" x 27".
Sew the strips together side by side to make a piece 6½" x 27".
    Press. Cut the piece into 6 pieces 4½" x 6½".

Leaves - Double:
Cut 2 Ivory strips 2½" x 18".
Sew the strips together side by side to make a piece 4½" x 18".
    Press. Cut the piece into 4 squares 4½" x 4½".

Leaves - Single:
Cut 6 Ivory strips 2½" x 4½".

Top of Middle Flower:
Cut 4 Ivory strips 2½" x 10½".
Sew the strips together side by side to make a piece
    8½" x 10½". Press.

Leaf Sections Assembly:
Sew the leaf-background sections into a column to form the right
    and left side of each stem section. Press.

Leaf and Stem Sections Assembly:
Sew a leaf column to the right and left side of each stem. Press.
    Make 2 long sections and 1 short section.

Flower Section

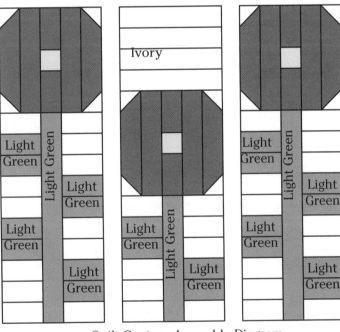

Quilt Center - Assembly Diagram

Flower Sections Assembly:
Sew long leaf and stem sections to flowers. Make 2.
Sew short leaf and stem sections to a flower. Make 1.
Sew 4 Ivory strips to the top of the short flower.

Ground Section:
    Cut 1 Tan and 3 Dark Green strips, each 2½" x 30½".
    Sew the strips together side by side,
        3 Green-Tan, to make a piece 8½" x 30½". Press.

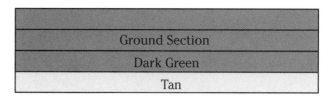

SEW BLOCKS:
Following the Quilt Center Assembly Diagram,
    arrange all the pieces on a work surface or
    table.

ASSEMBLY:
Arrange all Blocks on a work surface or table.
Refer to diagram for block placement and
    direction.
Sew the flower to the leaf-stem section. Press.
Sew the flower columns together. Press.
Sew the ground section to the bottom. Press.

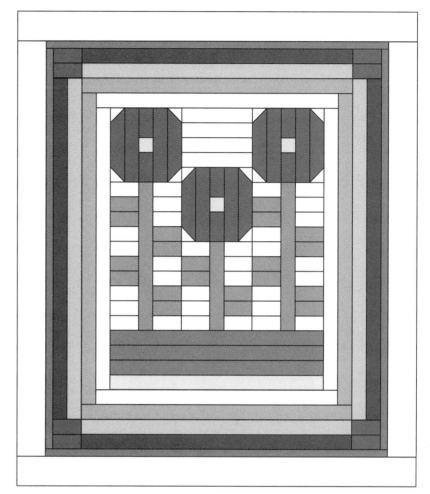

Natural Garden - Quilt Assembly Diagram

Ivory Pieced Border #1:
Cut 2½" Ivory print strips.
Sew strips together end to end.
Cut 2 strips 2½" x 38½" for sides.
Cut 2 strips 2½" x 34½" for top and bottom.
Sew side borders to the quilt.
    Press.
Sew top and bottom borders to the quilt.
    Press.

Tan Pieced Border #2:
Cut 2½" strips.
Sew Tan strips together end to end.
    Cut 2 strips 2½" x 42½" for sides.
    Cut 2 strips 2½" x 38½" for top and bottom.
    Sew side borders to the quilt. Press.
    Sew top and bottom borders to the quilt. Press.

Lavender-Purple Border #3:
Cut 2½" Purple strips.
For each color, sew Purple strips together end to end.
    Cut 2 Purple and 2 Lavender strips 2½" x 46½" for sides.
    Cut 2 Purple and 2 Lavender strips 2½" x 38½" for top and bottom.
    Cut 2 Red strips 18" long.
    Sew the Red strips together side by side. Press.
    Cut 4 Red 4½" x 4½" squares.
    Sew a Purple to a Lavender strip to make each border 4½" wide.
        Press.
    Sew side borders to the quilt. Press.
    Sew a Red square to each end of the top and bottom borders. Press.
    Sew top and bottom borders to the quilt. Press.

Dark Green Border #4:
Cut 1½" strips.
Sew Green strips together end to end.
    Cut 2 strips 1½" x 54½" for sides.
    Cut 2 strips 1½" x 48½" for top and bottom.
    Sew side borders to the quilt. Press.
    Sew top and bottom borders to the quilt. Press.

Ivory Border #5:
Cut 4½" strips.
Sew Ivory strips together end to end.
    Cut 2 strips 4½" x 56½" for sides.
    Cut 2 strips 4½" x 56½" for top and bottom.
    Sew side borders to the quilt. Press.
    Sew top and bottom borders to the quilt. Press.

FINISHING:
Quilting: See Basic Instructions on pages 24 - 27.
Binding: Cut six 2½" strips.
        Sew together end to end to equal 248".
        See Binding Instructions on page 27.

Friends & Flowers

photos on pages 50 - 51

SIZE: 48" x 72"
YARDAGE:
We used a *Moda* "Friends & Flowers" by Mary Engelbreit
   'Jelly Roll' collection of 2½" fabric strips
   - we purchased 1 'Jelly Roll'

⅓ yard Red	OR	4 strips
¼ yard Black	OR	2 strips
⅓ yard Yellow	OR	4 strips
⅜ yard Green	OR	5 strips
⅓ yard Blue	OR	4 strips
¾ yard White	OR	9 strips
⅓ yard Bias print	OR	4 strips
½ yard Stripe	OR	6 strips

Border #2   Purchase ½ yard Black polka dot
Border #3 & Binding   Purchase 1¾ yards Blue print
Backing   Purchase 3 yards
Batting   Purchase 56" x 80"
Sewing machine, needle, thread
DMC Pearl cotton (Black, Green, Red)
Optional: 6 Red buttons

HOUSE BLOCKS

Roof Section: 1
   Cut 3 Blue and 3 Black strips 6½" long.
   Sew the strips together side by side making a Blue square
      and a Black square, each 6½" x 6½".
   Place the squares right sides together.
   Follow the Half-Square Triangle instructions to the right.
   Make 2 Blue-Black squares and trim to 5½" x 5½".

Roof Section: 2
   Repeat these steps using Yellow and Black strips.

Roof:
   Following the diagram for color placement, sew 2 blocks
      together for each roof. Press.

House Sections:
   Cut 2 Yellow strips 1½" x 10½".
   Sew a strip to the bottom of each roof. Press.
   Cut 2½" wide strips in the following lengths:
      4 Red 12½",   4 Red 8½",   2 Red 6½", 4 Red 2½"
      2 Black 6½",   4 Black 2½"
   Arrange the pieces following the diagram.
   Sew the pieces together. Press.
   Sew the house section to the roof section. Press. Make 2.

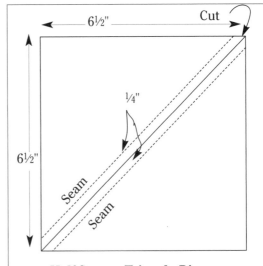

Half-Square Triangle Diagram
1. Place 2 squares right sides together.
2. Draw a diagonal line from corner to corner.
3. Stitch ¼" on each side of the line.
4. Cut squares apart on the diagonal line.
5. Open the 2 new squares with 2 colors.
6. Press. Trim off dog-ears.
7. Trim to 5½" x 5½".

Blue or Yellow

Blue or Yellow

Black

Make half-square triangles for the Roof

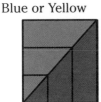

Black

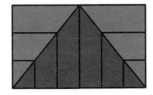

Roof Section

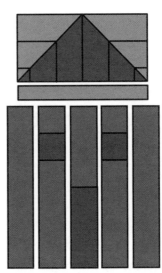
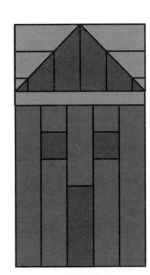

Center Row

BIRD BLOCK
  Cut 9 Ivory strips 2½" x 10½".
  Sew the strips together to make a piece 10½" x 18½".
  Press.

HEART BLOCK
  Cut 5 Yellow strips 2½" x 8½".
  Sew the strips together to make a piece 8½" x 10½".
  Press.

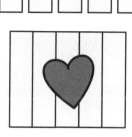

STAR BLOCK
Cut 3 Green strips 2½" x 22".
  Sew the strips together to make a piece 6½" x 22". Press.
  Center and trim to 5½" x 22".
  Cut the piece into 4 squares 5½" x 5½".

Cut 2 Yellow strips 1¼" x 5".
  Cut each strip into two triangles 1¼" x 5".

Follow the Star Diagram.
  Position a triangle on each Green square as shown
    (position and sew the LONG side to the pieced block).
  Sew and press.
Sew 4 squares together, 2 rows with 2 squares per row. Press.

Green

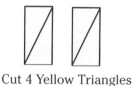

Cut 4 Yellow Triangles

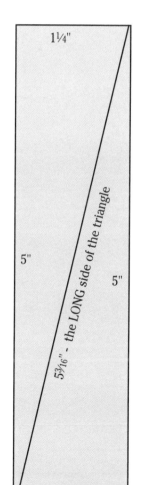

1¼"

5"

5"

5³/₁₆" - the LONG side of the triangle

1¼"

Pattern for
Yellow Triangles
Cut 4 triangles

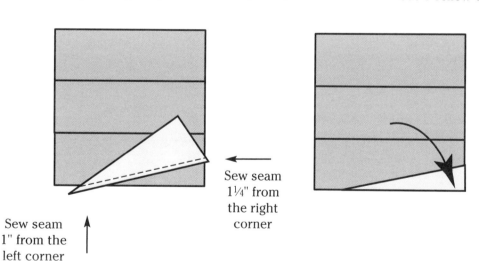

Sew seam
1¼" from
the right
corner

Sew seam
1" from the
left corner

Sew Gold Triangles to Green Squares
(Align the edges of each triangle as indicated on the diagram).

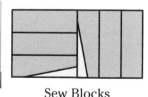

Sew Blocks
Make 2

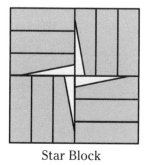

Star Block

continued on
page 40

BLUE BASKETS

Cut 6 Blue strips 2½" x 10½" and 2 Ivory 2½" x 2½" squares.
With right sides together, align a square on each end of
    1 Blue strip.
See Basket Diagram.
Draw a diagonal line on each White square and sew on the line.
Fold back the square to form a triangle.
Sew 3 strips together to make a piece 6½" x 10½". Press.
Make 2.

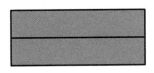

Sew 2 Blue strips together

BASKET BLOCK

Middle Row Basket Block

Cut 5 White strips 2½" x 12½".
Sew the strips together side by side to make a piece with
    vertical strips 10½" x 12½". Press.
Sew the basket to the White strips section. Press.

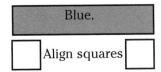

Align squares

Bottom Row Basket Block

Cut 6 White strips 2½" x 10½".
Sew the strips together side by side to make a piece with
    horizontal strips 10½" x 12½". Press.
Sew the basket to the White strip section. Press.

Sew on the diagonal

Bottom of basket

BIG SUNFLOWER

Big Flower:

Cut the following:
    1 Red square 2½" x 2½"
    4 White squares 2½" x 2½"
    4 Yellow strips 2½" x 10½"
    2 Yellow strips 2½" x 4½"

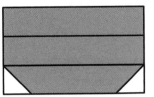

Sew Strips
to Make Basket

Flower Center:

Sew a Yellow 4½" strip - a Red square - a Yellow 4½" strip together. Press.

Flower Top and Bottom:

With right sides together, align a White square on each end of
2 Yellow 2½" x 10½" strips.
Draw a diagonal line on each square and sew on the line.
Fold back each square to form a triangle on the end of each strip. Press.

Flower:

Arrange the pieces following the diagram.
Sew the 5 Yellow and Yellow pieced strips together to make a
10½" x 10½" square with horizontal strips. Press.

Flower Top:

Cut 2 White strips 2½" x 10½".
Sew strips together side by side.

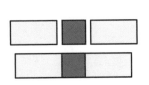

Flower Center

Yellow

Align squares and sew

Flower Top and Bottom

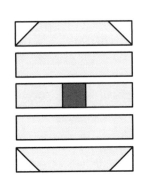

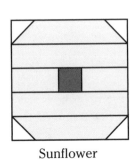

Sunflower

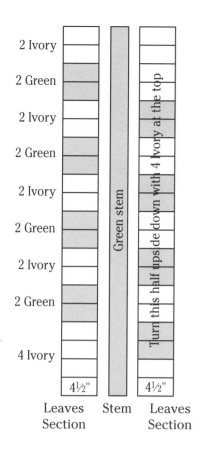

2 Ivory
2 Green
2 Ivory
2 Green
2 Ivory
2 Green
2 Ivory
2 Green
4 Ivory

4½"

Leaves Section

Green stem

Stem

Turn this half upside down with 4 Ivory at the top

4½"

Leaves Section

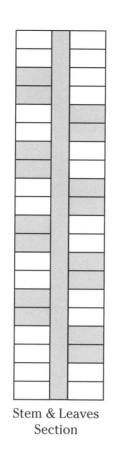

Stem & Leaves Section

Stem and Leaves:
> Cut the following lengths of 2½" wide strips:
> > 1 Green 40½" for the long stem,
> > 8 Green 9",
> > 12 Ivory print 9"
> Arrange the pieces following the diagram:
> > 2 Ivory - 2 Green - 2 Ivory - 2 Green
> > 2 Ivory - 2 Green - 2 Ivory - 2 Green - 4 Ivory
> Sew the strips together. Press.
> Cut 2 strips, each 4½" x 40½".

Assemble Stem and Leaves:
> Arrange the pieces following the diagram:
> > 1 Leaves section - 1 Stem - 1 Leaves section
> > (turn 1 stem upside down)
> Sew the strips together. Press.

Assemble Stem, Leaves and Sunflower:
> Sew the Sunflower to the stem section. Press.

ASSEMBLY:
> Arrange all Blocks on a work surface or table.
> Refer to diagram for placement and direction.
> Sew blocks together in 3 columns. Press.
> Sew the columns together. Press.

continued on page 42

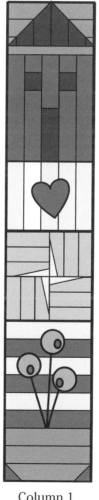

Column 1

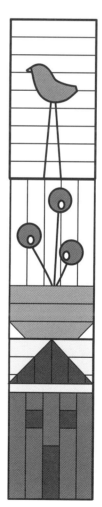

Column 2

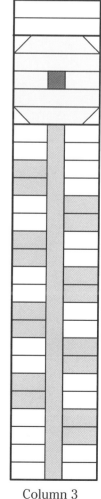

Column 3

BORDERS:

Pieced Border #1:

Preparing the pieces:

Cut leftover White print strips into
6½" to 12½" assorted lengths.

Sew strips end to end to make a
very long strip.

Press.

Sewing the strips:

Side Rows:

Cut into 4 strips, each 54½" long.

Sew 2 strips to the left side.

Sew 2 strips to the right side.

Press.

Top and Bottom Rows:

Cut into 4 strips, each 38½" long.

Sew 2 strips to the top.

Sew 2 strips to the bottom.

Press.

Border #2:

Cut 1½" strips.

Sew strips together end to end.

Cut 2 strips 1½" x 62½" for sides.

Cut 2 strips 1½" x 40½" for top and
bottom.

Sew side borders to the quilt. Press.

Sew top and bottom borders to the quilt.
Press.

Border #3:

Cut 4½" strips.

Sew strips together end to end.

Cut 2 strips 4½" x 64½" for sides.

Cut 2 strips 4½" x 48½" for top and
bottom.

Sew side borders to the quilt. Press.

Sew top and bottom borders to the quilt.
Press.

Optional Applique:

Cut 2 Red strips 2½" x 20".

Sew strips together to make a piece 4½" x 20".

Trace and cut out 1 heart and 6 flowers.

Cut 2 Blue strips 2½" x 6".

Sew strips together to make a piece 4½" x 6".

Trace and cut out 1 bird.

Trace and cut beak from Yellow scrap.

Follow the Basic Instructions for Applique on page 26.

FINISHING:

Quilting:

See Basic Instructions on pages 26 - 28.

Binding:

Cut six 2½" strips.

Sew together end to end to equal 248".

See Binding Instructions on page 27.

Buttons:

Sew a button to each flower center after quilting.

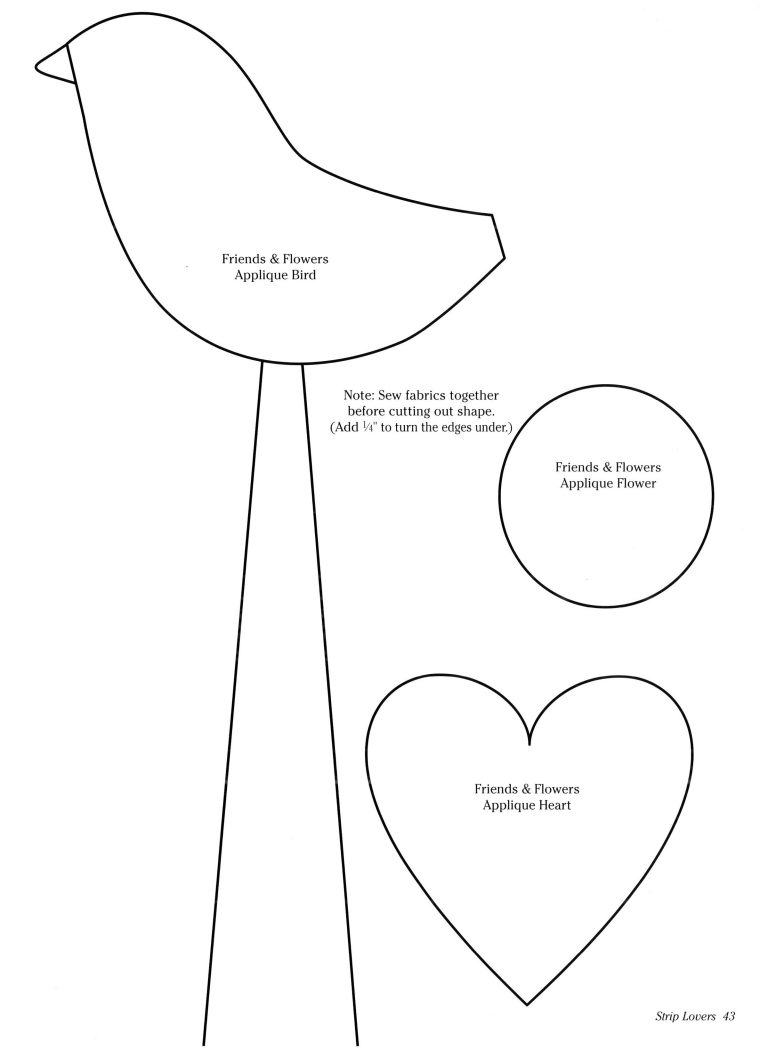

Friends & Flowers
Applique Bird

Note: Sew fabrics together
before cutting out shape.
(Add ¼" to turn the edges under.)

Friends & Flowers
Applique Flower

Friends & Flowers
Applique Heart

Strawberry Lemonade

pieced by Donna Perrotta
quilted by Julie Lawson
Zesty and bright, Strawberry Lemonade zings with
life, color and energy. These zigzags are surprisingly
simple to piece and the strip technique generates the
fabulous random look of this fruity quilt.

instructions on pages 28 - 31

Maypole

pieced by Donna Perrotta
quilted by Julie Lawson

Swirling colors of Spring and Summer dance across this energetic quilt. Toss this one over your favorite reading chair on the porch to keep away the evening chill and brighten your afternoons.

instructions on pages 32 - 35

Suzanne McNeill

"I love designing ... painting, crafting and working with fabrics. The colors, feel and textures are exciting.

Quilts are my favorite!"

Suzanne

Suzanne shares her creativity and enthusiasm in books by Design Originals. Her 'best-selling Strip Happy' quilt books are known for their simple construction and colorful designs.

Suzanne's mission is to publish books that help others learn about the newest techniques, the best projects and most popular products.

Natural Garden

pieced by
Donna Perrotta
quilted by
Julie Lawson

Quilter, quilter, how does your garden grow? Naturally, with blossoms all year around!

This beautiful quilt is a blooming choice for everyone who loves flowers or gardening.

instructions on
pages 36 - 37